Take a trip to
LEBANON

Richard Tames

Franklin Watts

London   New York   Sydney   Toronto

Facts about Lebanon

Area:
10,400 sq. km.
(4,010 sq. miles)

Population:
3,320,000

Capital:
Beirut

Largest Cities:
Beirut (702,000)
Tripoli (175,000)
Zahle (47,000)
Sidon (25,000)
Tyre (14,000)

Official language:
Arabic

Religions:
Islam, Christianity

Main Exports:
Gold and coins; fruit and
vegetables; textiles

Currency:
Lebanese pound

Franklin Watts
12a Golden Square
London W1

Franklin Watts Inc.
387 Park Avenue South
New York, N.Y. 10016

ISBN: UK Edition 0 86 313 810 1
ISBN: US Edition 0–531–10652–7
Library of Congress Catalog Card No:
88-51324
© Franklin Watts Limited 1989

Typeset by Lineage, Watford
Printed in Hong Kong

Maps: Simon Roulestone
Design: Edward Kinsey

Stamps: Stanley Gibbons Limited
Photographs: Chris Fairclough 8;
Hutchison Library 4, 5, 7, 10, 11, 12, 13,
16, 17, 18, 20, 21, 27; Christine Osborne 3,
6, 15, 19, 22, 23, 24, 25, 26, 28, 29, 30, 31;
ZEFA 14

Front and Back Cover:
Christine Osborne

Lebanon is a small, mountainous country, lying along the eastern coast of the Mediterranean Sea. These fishing boats at the port of Tripoli remind us that the sea has played an important part in the history of this trading nation.

Behind the narrow coastal plain are the Lebanon Mountains. The highest peak, Qurnat as Sawda, which is in northern Lebanon, reaches 3,083m (10,115 ft) in height. In the past, many people have found safety from harsh governments in Lebanon's mountains.

The Anti-Lebanon mountain range runs along Lebanon's eastern border with Syria. A train journey through the mountains takes passengers from one capital, Beirut, in Lebanon, to another, Damascus, in Syria. The mountains have snowy winters and cool summers.

The largest area of flat land in Lebanon is the Bekaa Valley, between the Lebanon and Anti-Lebanon ranges. It is warmer and drier than the mountains. It has many vineyards and wheatfields. Two important rivers, the Orontes and Litani flow through the Bekaa Valley.

The Litani River, flowing south from the Bekaa Valley, turns west through a deep gorge in the Lebanon Mountains on its way to the sea. Near the point where the river turns west is the castle of Beaufort.

7

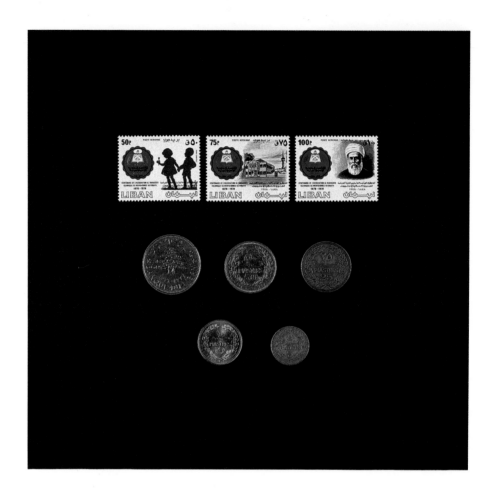

The picture shows some of the money and stamps used in Lebanon. The main unit of currency is the pound, which is divided into 100 piastres.

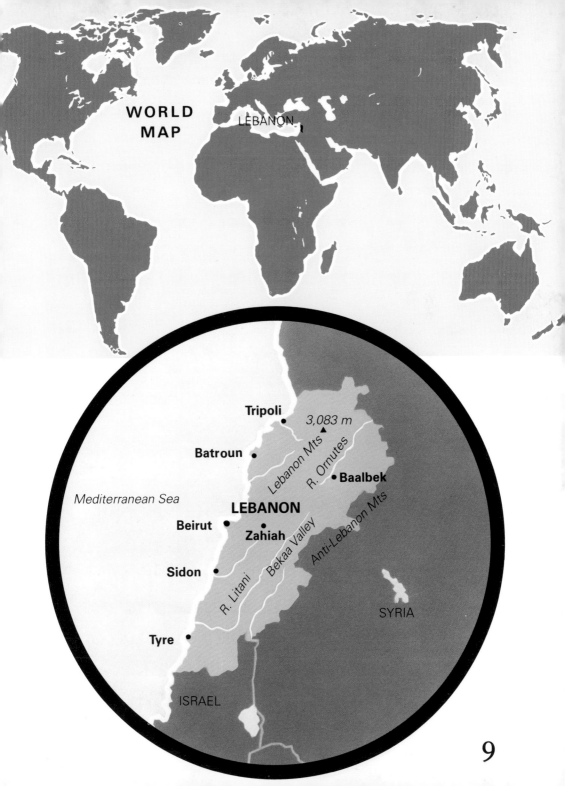

WORLD
MAP

LEBANON

Tripoli
3,083 m
Batroun
Lebanon Mts
R. Ornutes
Baalbek
Mediterranean Sea
LEBANON
Beirut
Zahiah
Sidon
R. Litani
Bekaa Valley
Anti-Lebanon Mts
SYRIA
Tyre
ISRAEL

9

Trade has been important in Lebanon since ancient times. By 1000 BC, an ancient sea-faring people, the Phoenicians, had built a great empire around the Mediterranean Sea based on the ports of Tyre and Sidon. Byblos, shown above, is an even older port.

For centuries, Lebanon was an important part of the Roman Empire. At Baalbek, in the northern Bekaa Valley, the Romans built great temples for their gods, Jupiter and Bacchus.

Christianity came to Lebanon in about AD 335. Lebanon was then part of the eastern Roman Empire ruled from Byzantium. Most Lebanese Christians belong to the Maronite Church, which is named after Maro, a Syrian saint. It follows Roman Catholic teachings, but has its own priests.

The Arabs conquered Lebanon in the 7th century. They brought the Arabic language and their religion, Islam. Arabic is now Lebanon's official language and more than half the people are Muslims — followers of Islam. This mosque, where Muslims worship, is in Byblos.

During the 12th and 13th centuries, Christian Crusaders fought the Muslims for control of the country. The Crusaders built this "sea castle" at Sidon in 1227. The Muslims seized the castle in 1291, and soon afterwards the Crusaders gave up trying to conquer Lebanon.

Arabs account for about 90 per cent of the population. Armenians form the largest minority group. Lebanon also has some Kurds, Assyrians, Jews, Greeks and Turks. The picture shows some Bedouin Arabs, who used to lead a nomadic (wandering) way of life.

   The people of Lebanon are divided by
religion. There are two main groups of
Muslims: the Sunni and the Shiite
Muslims, who have some different
beliefs. The poster of Ayatollah
Khomeini, the leader of Iran, where most
people are Shiites, shows that this
Lebanese village is also peopled by
Shiites.

The Druses, who form a community of about 100,000, follow a religion which grew out of Islam. Its secret beliefs are guarded by people like this Druse elder. The Druses keep themselves separate from both Muslims and Christians.

The government of Lebanon is organized so that both Christians and Muslims share power. In 1975 religious and other divisions between the people led to a civil war. Each main group in Lebanon now has its own soldiers to protect it from other groups.

Foreign troops from Syria and Israel have entered Lebanon in support of different groups during Lebanon's continuing civil war. A UN peace keeping force has also been involved. The picture shows damage to buildings in Beirut, the capital, caused by fighting.

In the 1970s, almost 200,000 Palestinian refugees lived in Lebanon. The guerilla fighters of the Palestine Liberation Organization, or PLO, who are opposed to Israel, left Lebanon after the Israelis invaded in 1982. But thousands of Palestinian refugees remain. They live in camps in poor conditions.

Israel invaded southern Lebanon in order to destroy bases used by the PLO. But the Israelis felt unable to leave until 1985, when they agreed to arm Christian militia forces guarding the Lebanon-Israel border.

Lebanon's mountains have a good rainfall by Middle Eastern standards. Fruit growing is important, and apples are the leading crop. Melons, citrus fruits, tobacco, vegetables, wheat and olives are also cultivated, especially in the Bekaa Valley.

Farming employs about a tenth of Lebanon's workers. This farmer is driving a load of sugar-beet. Modern machinery makes it easier for farmers to manage with fewer workers. But Lebanon still imports some of its food.

Farmland covers about a third of the country. The men in the picture are pruning vines. The grapes will be made into wine. Grazing by goats has damaged the country's forests and Lebanon is less green than it used to be.

Despite the civil war, Lebanon still carries on much trade through Beirut and its other ports. But the importance of world banking in Lebanon has declined. The country's oil refineries, as well as many factories, have closed down.

Lebanon is famous for its arts and crafts. Beautiful objects were once made for wealthy merchants and landowners. In modern times tourists have kept up the demand for textiles or hand-made metal wares. This craftsman in the picture is only 12 years old.

Tourism was a major industry until the outbreak of civil war. Lebanon has many attractions. Visitors could ski in the mountains and then go swimming in the sea after a half hour's drive. Other attractions include historic sites and superb food.

The Lebanese have always been good at business both at home and abroad. Although the civil war has made it difficult to plan ahead, many small businesses, such as this shop selling olives and other groceries, have kept going.

Family ties are strong in Lebanon, but the difficult times of the 1970s and 1980s have made them even more important. Many families, such as this Christian family, which has come together for a meal, have relatives abroad who send them money and other things they need.

The Lebanese are the most highly educated people in the Arab world. Four out of every five can read and write. There are about 40 daily newspapers. Most are in Arabic but three are in Armenian, three in French and two in English.

Primary education is free. This boy is learning to write in Arabic. Well-educated children like him are Lebanon's best hope for the future. If Lebanon could once again have a stable government, it might, once more, become a prosperous country.

Index